QUEEN ELIZABETH

(Courtesy of Andrew Sassoli-Walker)

QUEEN ELIZABETH

A Photographic Journey

CHRIS FRAME AND RACHELLE CROSS
WITH A CAPTAIN'S PERSPECTIVE BY CAPTAIN CHRIS WELLS

For Aaron, Ben, Catherine & Alex

Paperback published 2015

First published 2011

The History Press

The Mill

Brimscombe Port

Stroud

Gloucestershire

GL5 2QG

www.thehistorypress.co.uk

British Library Cataloguing in Publication Data.
A catalogue record for this book is available from the British Library.

ISBN 978-0-7509-6305-3

Typesetting and origination by The History Press Ltd

Printed in China

Back cover: Image courtesy of John Frame.

CONTENTS

FOREWORD

BY PETER SHANKS
FORMER PRESIDENT OF CUNARD LINE

In October 2010 Cunard welcomed to its fleet the third liner in its 170-year history bearing the name *Queen Elizabeth*.

The first *Queen Elizabeth* was launched by Her Majesty Queen Elizabeth, the late Queen Mother, in the presence of her daughters, the Princesses Elizabeth and Margaret, in 1938. That ship was the largest passenger liner ever built until the arrival of *Queen Mary 2* in 2003. Following a secret dash across the Atlantic after the outbreak of war, *Queen Elizabeth* served her country with distinction. When she finally entered commercial service in 1946 she and her sister *Queen Mary* epitomised the golden age of transatlantic travel until their retirements in the late 1960s.

Peter Shanks examines a model of *Queen Elizabeth*. (Courtesy Michael Gallagher/Cunard)

The next Elizabeth – *Queen Elizabeth 2* – thundered down the slipway into the River Clyde after her launch by Her Majesty the Queen in 1967. *QE2*'s place in maritime history is forever assured after her outstanding thirty-nine-year career which saw her not only sail over 5 million nautical miles, more than any other ship, but also become the longest-serving Cunard transatlantic liner ever.

HM Queen Elizabeth II at the ship's christening. (Michael Gallagher/ Cunard)

Queen Elizabeth arrives in Southampton for the first time. (Courtesy Andrew Sassoli-Walker)

The third *Queen Elizabeth* is a beautiful and gracious vessel and is a sister to the widely acclaimed *Queen Victoria*. She does, however, have her own distinct personality and is the second largest Cunarder ever built.

We were both honoured and proud that Her Majesty named our new Queen in Southampton on Monday 11 October 2010. The event was a milestone in British maritime history and was a major event of worldwide interest.

I was delighted to point out during the ceremony that Her Majesty was the only person present who attended all three Elizabeth launches. She was there at the age of twelve at the launch of the first *Queen Elizabeth* on 27 September 1938 when she accompanied her mother, Queen Elizabeth, to Clydebank for the launch. Her Majesty herself launched *QE2* on 20 September 1967.

The new *Queen Elizabeth* will take this historic name far into the twenty-first century and will ensure the success of Cunard Line for many years to come.

ACKNOWLEDGEMENTS

We are extremely grateful to everyone who helped us share this photographic journey aboard *Queen Elizabeth*.

Special thanks to: **Peter Shanks**, President of Cunard Line, for writing the foreword; **Captain Chris Wells**, Master of *Queen Elizabeth*, for sharing with us the captain's perspective; **Captain Julian Burgess** for participating in an 'on the bridge' interview for the previous edition; **Commodore Rynd** for sharing his thoughts on *Queen Elizabeth* on her fifth anniversary.

Our thanks goes to **Michael Gallagher**, Cunard Historian, for helping organise content and imagery; **Alastair Greener**, former Entertainment Director aboard *Queen Elizabeth*, for his perspective of the entertainment aboard, as well as helping us access areas 'behind the scenes'; and all of the *Queen Elizabeth* officers and crew who accommodated us aboard while preparing this book and taking photographs.

We are extremely grateful to **Amy Rigg**, **Emily Locke**, **Glad Stockdale**, **Chrissy McMorris** and everyone at The History Press for their ongoing support.

We'd like to thank **David Webster** and the team at Cunard Insights for their ongoing support of our maritime lectures; and our thanks to **Bill Miller** for his continued support and assistance. Thank you to **Andrew Sassoli-Walker**, **Ian Boyle** (Simplon Post Cards), **Jan Frame**, **John Frame** and **John Hargreaves** for their photographic assistance; and our families for supporting us.

All photographs unless otherwise credited were taken by Chris Frame or Rachelle Cross.

Top left: (Courtesy of Jan Frame)
Below: (Courtesy of Andrew Sassoli-Walker)

Queen Elizabeth

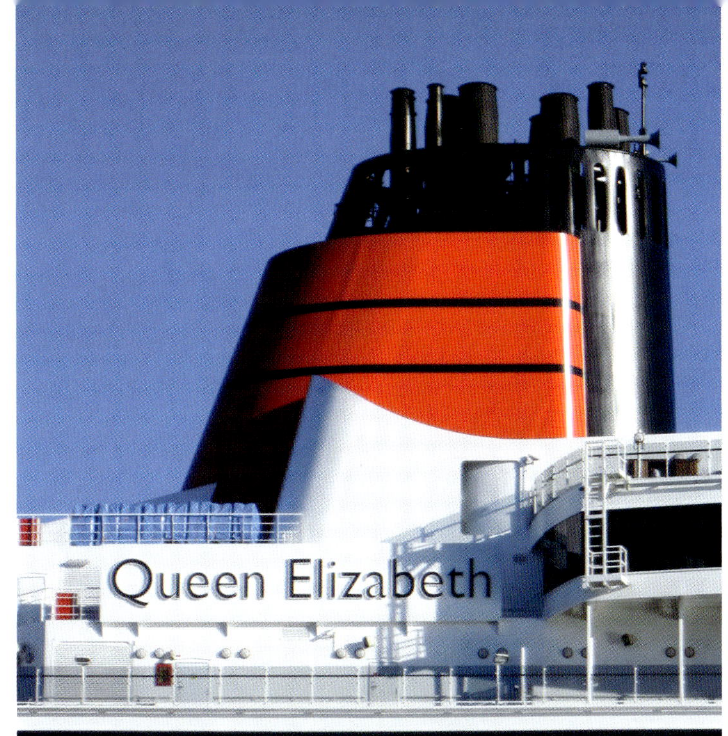

Queen Elizabeth

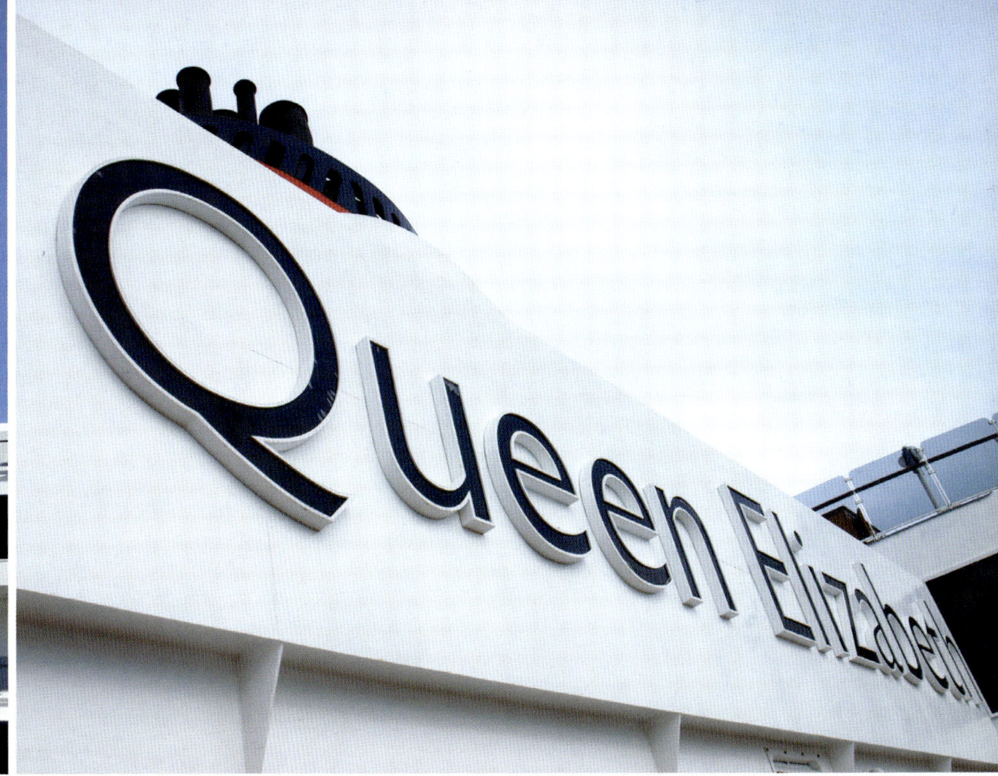

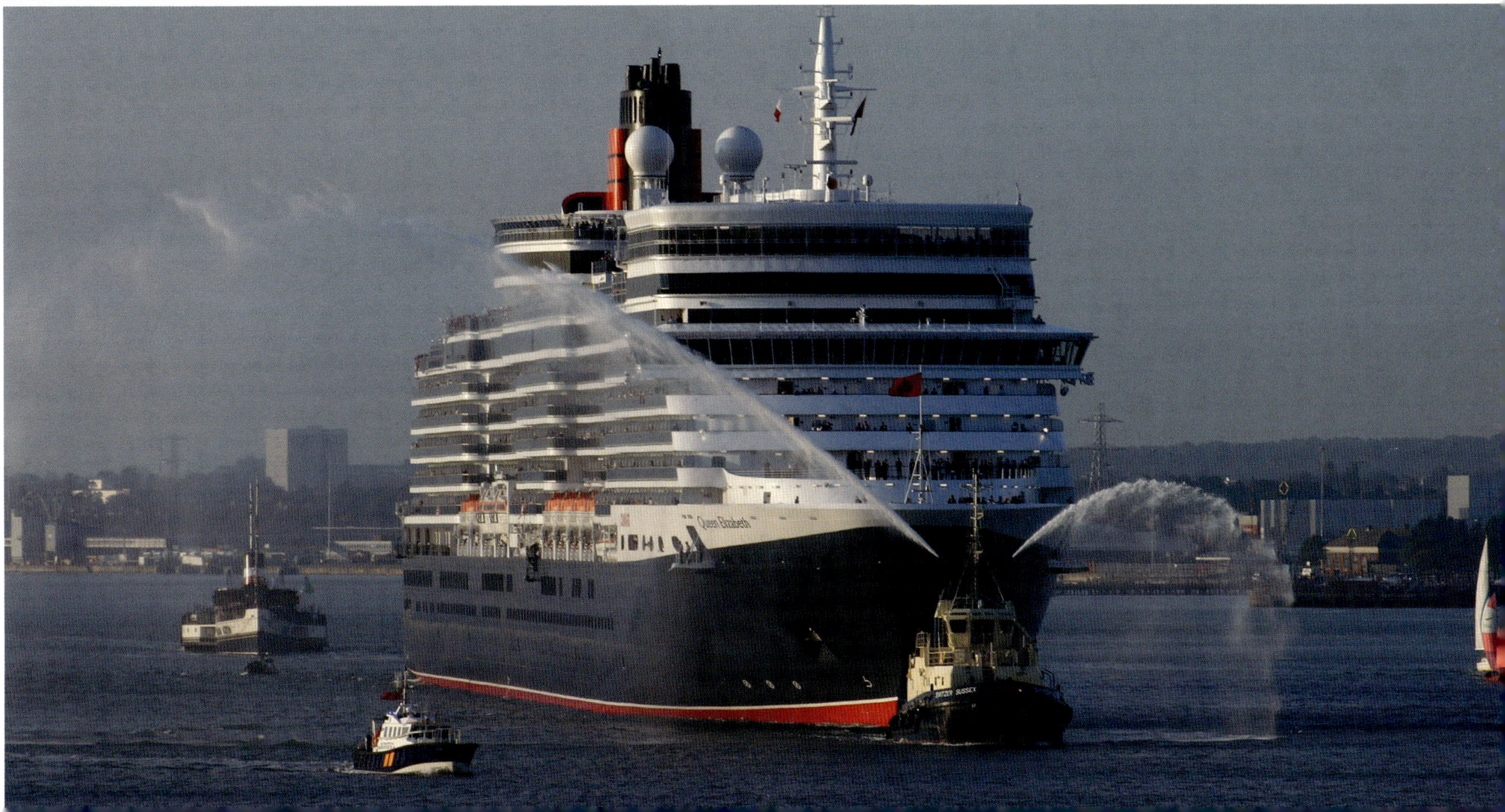
Queen Elizabeth

A ROYAL INTRODUCTION

The *Queen Elizabeth* represents the coming of age for the modern-day Cunard Line. The second vista-class Queen, she is the third Cunarder to be named Elizabeth. Her name alone affords her a special significance within the history of the Cunard Line, for she continues the traditions set down by two of the greatest ocean liners of all time, the legendary *Queen Elizabeth* of 1940, and the immortal *Queen Elizabeth 2* of 1969.

Today's *Queen Elizabeth* is a very different ship than her predecessors. Built for the modern age, she concentrates mainly on pleasure cruises, leaving the rigour of the transatlantic crossing (Cunard's traditional sea passage) to her ocean liner fleet mate *Queen Mary 2*. Despite this, *Queen Elizabeth* is no mere cruise ship. A strengthened hull allows her to undertake transcontinental sea routes, such as the transatlantic crossing, a voyage she first undertook in tandem with *Queen Victoria* in January 2011.

Inside, *Queen Elizabeth* represents the best of twenty-first-century comforts, while in a tribute to the original *Queen Elizabeth*, her interior design invokes the beauty of one of the most memorable twentieth-century styles, Art Deco.

Further tributes to her predecessors exist on board, which will delight past Cunard passengers while offering new guests the opportunity to learn more about the company's rich heritage. Some of the most talked about items are on loan from *QE2* and once formed part of the Cunard Heritage Trail aboard that ship.

This sixth Cunard Queen will ensure Cunard's ongoing success well into the twenty-first century, while ensuring the name Elizabeth continues to be one of the most famous words in the passenger shipping dictionary.

***Queen Elizabeth* in Southampton. (Courtesy Michael Gallagher/Cunard)**

DID YOU KNOW?

Queen Elizabeth was built at Fincantieri shipyard in Italy. In accordance with Italian tradition the ship was given a Madrina (Italian for godmother) when being built. *Queen Elizabeth*'s Madrina is Dennie Farmer.

LOOKING BACK

Cunard Line has had many famous names over nearly two centuries of operation. Safe, reliable service during both war and peace has resulted in ships such as *Britannia*, *Mauretania*, *Aquitania*, *Caronia* and *Queen Mary* becoming household names. Despite this enviable lineage, the name *Queen Elizabeth* holds special significance.

The first *Queen Elizabeth* was constructed at the brink of one of the darkest times in history. A sister ship to the already famous *Queen Mary*, the new Cunarder, then known as Hull 552, became the largest passenger ship in the world, a title she retained for many decades.

Launched at the John Brown shipyard in 1938 and named in honour of Elizabeth Bowes-Lyon, Queen Consort to King George VI (later to become the Queen Mother), the ship was christened by HM the Queen herself in front of thousands of spectators. However, despite the celebrations, the shadow of war was ever-present and by the time the new Cunarder was ready to enter service, Britain was already embroiled in a fierce fight for survival.

Queen Mary. (Courtesy of Ian Boyle / Simplon Post Cards)

Queen Elizabeth started her service life as a troop carrier, making hundreds of voyages carrying Allied troops to the war zone. Fortunately, she was able to escape the conflict unscathed. Her admirable service to King and Country gained her a reputation not dissimilar to that of a national hero.

During the late 1940s and 1950s, *Queen Elizabeth* enjoyed fame and glory as one of the two most prestigious ocean liners on the iconic transatlantic route. Weekly crossings included the highlight of passing sister ship *Queen Mary* mid-voyage as the two Queens made their way to their respective ports at a combined speed of over 60 knots.

QE2 and *Queen Elizabeth* in Dubai, 2011. (Courtesy Michael Gallagher/ Cunard)

Despite their speed and comforts, by the 1960s international travel had changed significantly. The Queens were made redundant with the introduction of affordable jet air travel and by the mid-1960s *Queen Elizabeth* was sailing as a ghost ship. Cunard had no alternative but to retire her.

All was not lost, however, as the Cunard Line had plans for a new breed of passenger liner. This new ship, code-named Number 736, was built at the same shipyard as her predecessor and was expected to take the same name, *Queen Elizabeth*, upon her launch in 1967.

The second Elizabeth was christened by HM Queen Elizabeth II who personally altered the ship's name to '*Queen Elizabeth the Second*', and thus *QE2* was born.

The *QE2*, forerunner of *Queen Elizabeth*. (Courtesy Michael Gallagher/Cunard)

QE2 would capture the hearts and minds of a whole new generation of traveller. She was trendy, modern and exciting. She became an instant hit. Smaller than the previous *Queen Elizabeth*, *QE2* could transit the Panama Canal, allowing her to travel to ports all over the globe and offer a holiday-style alternative to travelling by jet.

QE2 had a long and interesting life. In fact, by the time she retired in November 2008, she had travelled over 5 million miles, carrying more than 2.5 million passengers, and earning herself the crown as the most famous ship in the world.

Her career saw her answer the call of duty during the Falklands War, transporting some 3,000 troops from Southampton to Cumberland Bay. She went on to carry royalty, dignitaries and celebrities, participate in naval reviews and twice operate as a chartered floating hotel, just to name a few of her accomplishments.

It was not long after *QE2*'s retirement was announced that Cunard stated their intention to build a new *Queen Elizabeth*. This third Elizabeth became Cunard's sixth Queen and her keel was laid down at the Fincantieri shipyard in Italy in July 2009.

A near sister to *Queen Victoria* and running mate to *QM2*, *Queen Elizabeth* entered service in October 2010. She pays homage to her namesakes, not only sharing their famous name, but also aspects of their interior spaces. Her décor is unmistakably Art Deco in style, a tribute to the original *Queen Elizabeth*, while rooms such as the Queens Room and the Yacht Club take their names from *QE2*.

Queen Elizabeth is a fine Cunarder, a ship with an enviable pedigree behind her. She has the proud traditions and heritage of the first *Queen Elizabeth* as well as *QE2* to maintain. However, she also enjoys a bright future, as she sails the globe gaining fame and affection all over the world, much like her namesakes did before her.

Long live the Queen!

WELCOME ABOARD

Cunard's first *Queen Elizabeth*, launched in 1938, was decorated in Art Deco style. That style is echoed in the fit out of Cunard's new *Queen Elizabeth*.

The three-storey Grand Lobby is dominated by a 5.6m-high marquetry screen created by David Linley, which depicts the first *Queen Elizabeth* in nine different woods. A stunning Art Deco chandelier hangs from the ceiling of Deck 4 and highlights the curved theme of the balconies and three double staircases below.

The lobby is decorated in a range of warm browns and creams which gives the room a welcoming feel despite its size and grandeur.

David Linley's mural of the original *Queen Elizabeth* in the Grand Lobby.

ACCOMMODATION ABOARD

At the end of a busy day on board or on shore, *Queen Elizabeth*'s staterooms are a fantastic place to relax, unwind and catch up on your beauty sleep. With room service available 24 hours a day, a wide variety of channels on the television and attentive and friendly cabin stewards, your cabin soon feels like your home away from home.

More than 70 per cent of *Queen Elizabeth*'s cabins feature balconies, which are an ideal spot to appreciate the pleasure of being at sea. Watching the ocean slip past from the seclusion of your private balcony is the ideal start and end to a day aboard *Queen Elizabeth*.

Like the other Cunard ships, cabins aboard *Queen Elizabeth* are graded by luxury and the various cabin grades correspond to the dining room you eat in.

Since 2014, *Queen Elizabeth* has offered nine single cabins for passengers travelling alone.

QUEENS GRILL ACCOMMODATION

The *Queen Elizabeth*'s premium accommodation grade is Queens Grill. The Queens Grill staterooms are located over Decks 3 to 8 and are all spacious and luxurious. In addition to being the largest staterooms aboard, the Queens Grill accommodation also offers the most extras.

Those staying in Queens Grill accommodation receive the attention of a butler in addition to the Grills Concierge available to both Princess and Queens Grill passengers. Fresh flowers and fruit are provided in room for these passengers.

The six Grand and Master suites are the best of the best. These six staterooms have been named after the six Cunard Commodores who have been knighted.

PRINCESS GRILL ACCOMMODATION

Princess Grill guests stay in luxurious suites which are found on Decks 3 to 8. Each of these staterooms has a sitting area which can be used for entertaining and a balcony for private relaxation.

Passengers staying in Princess Grill accommodation have access to the private Grills Lounge, Courtyard and Terrace, as well as the assistance of the Grills Concierge.

BRITANNIA CLUB ACCOMMODATION

If you crave extra luxuries without the price tag associated with the Grill Class experience, then the Britannia Club is for you! All Britannia Club staterooms have spacious balconies and are located exclusively on Deck 8.

With sizes ranging between 22.5m² to 43.8m² (242ft² to 472ft²), Britannia Club passengers will enjoy extra amenities, such as the nine choices on the Pillow Concierge menu for a perfect night's sleep.

Britannia Club passengers have their own restaurant located just forward of the main Britannia dining room.

DID YOU KNOW?

In keeping with the *Queen Elizabeth*'s style, the daily programme aboard *Queen Elizabeth* has an Art Deco design, making it unique from the other Cunard daily programmes.

BRITANNIA ACCOMMODATION

Britannia accommodation aboard *Queen Elizabeth* ranges from modest inside cabins to spacious staterooms with balconies. Regardless of the size, you'll find these rooms comfortable and relaxing.

Situated across a variety of decks, Britannia is the most popular cabin category aboard. These cabins all come with twin beds (convertible to a Queen), along with en-suite bathrooms and a desk and chair for writing.

With Cunard's signature 24-hour room service, you can enjoy a snack or a full meal in the comfort of your own home away from home, no matter what time of day!

RESTAURANTS ABOARD

Fine food is easy to come by aboard *Queen Elizabeth*. Guests are assigned to one of four formal dining venues based on their cabin grade. Each of these restaurants offers an ever-changing menu in a beautiful location. The service is friendly and efficient and most guests choose to eat at their assigned restaurant every evening.

For those who prefer variety in their dining location or prefer a more relaxed atmosphere there are a number of alternative dining venues aboard as well. The Lido and Lido Pool Grill offer buffet-style dining, while the Verandah on Deck 2 offers a completely different menu for those who choose to eat here.

RESTAURANT PROFILE

Restaurant	Location	Seatings
Queens Grill	Deck 11	Single Seating
Princess Grill	Deck 11	Single Seating
Britannia Club	Deck 2	Single Seating
Britannia Restaurant	Decks 2 & 3	Double Seating
The Lido	Deck 9	Open Buffet/Single Seating
The Lido Pool Grill	Deck 9	Open Grill
The Verandah	Deck 2	Single Seating

QUEENS GRILL

The Grills Lounge on Deck 11 is the entry point for the Queens Grill restaurant on the port side of this deck. This restaurant is the main dining venue for those passengers travelling in the most exclusive grade of accommodation aboard the ship and the restaurant does not disappoint.

With a gold colour palate complemented by the stained-glass windows on the inner walls of the restaurant, this room offers the feeling of an intimate dining location whilst still allowing for a spectacular feeling of space courtesy of the full-size windows along the port side of the room.

Those who dine in the Queens Grill are also given the option of dining outdoors in the private Courtyard, which is located aft of the Grills Lounge.

PRINCESS GRILL

The Princess Grill is located on the starboard side of Deck 11 and is accessed from the Grills Lounge. Princess Grill diners are treated to luxurious surroundings with artworks and murals scattered about the restaurant.

Varied menus and excellent service provide a superb dining experience for those passengers travelling in this class. Princess Grill passengers, like those in the Queens Grill, can also choose to take meals in the sheltered Courtyard between the two restaurants.

DID YOU KNOW?

Queen Elizabeth celebrated five years in service in October 2015.

BRITANNIA CLUB

Located on Deck 2, just forward of the Britannia Restaurant, you'll find *Queen Elizabeth*'s Britannia Club.

A popular dining venue aboard flagship *QM2*, the Britannia Club was included on *Queen Elizabeth* in a space occupied by the Chartroom Bar aboard her sister ship *Queen Victoria*.

This restaurant is the main dining room for those passengers travelling Britannia Club class. Though not as dramatic as the Britannia Restaurant, the Britannia Club Restaurant is an attractive dining venue with features including ocean liner-patterned glass panels along the inner wall and large windows offering views of the ocean along the starboard wall. Decorated in *Queen Elizabeth*'s hallmark Art Deco style, the restaurant offers single-seating dining for breakfast, lunch and dinner.

BRITANNIA RESTAURANT

Like the *QM2* and *Queen Victoria*, *Queen Elizabeth*'s main dining room, which caters to the majority of passengers aboard, is called the Britannia Restaurant.

The entrance to the double-height Britannia Restaurant is dominated by a dramatic curved double staircase and eye-catching Art Deco lighting, including a low-hanging chandelier. The central focus of the room is a huge arched partition with an Art Deco motif that offers a modern take on the style and grace found aboard the original Queens.

The Britannia Restaurant is located at the aft of Decks 2 and 3 and offers spectacular views of the ocean to those with a table on the starboard side or aft of the restaurant.

Guests are catered to in an open-seating arrangement at breakfast and lunch times and in a set arrangement at dinner. Due to the number of passengers who make use of the Britannia Restaurant at dinner there are two seatings, one at 6 p.m. and the other at 8.30 p.m.

THE LIDO

If you're looking for a casual dining experience for breakfast, lunch or dinner, as well as a constant stream of snacks, you'll love the Lido restaurant on Deck 9. The restaurant serves food buffet style, with two buffet lines in addition to a 'made to order' section. The offerings change daily throughout your voyage, though there are some favourites available every day.

The restaurant is decorated in Art Deco style, with large windows on both sides allowing diners to appreciate the view. Its light and airy atmosphere, casual ambiance and open seating makes the Lido a popular alternative to the formal restaurants.

In the evenings the Lido restaurant offers a number of extra tariff options in addition to the buffet. These options are based around regional cuisines and are named similarly. Sections of the Lido are closed off and those partaking of this offering are given table service in these temporary dining zones.

The three extra tariff options available on a nightly basis are Azteca for Mexican food, Asado for South American food and Jasmine for Asian food.

DID YOU KNOW?

Six Cunard Commodores have been knighted throughout the company's history. They are: Commodore Sir James Charles, Commodore Sir Arthur Rostron, Commodore Sir Edgar Britten, Commodore Sir James Bisset, Commodore Sir Cyril Illingworth and Commodore Sir Ivan Thompson.

THE LIDO POOL GRILL

For a truly relaxed dining experience the Lido Pool Grill on the aft end of Deck 9 offers it all. The casual buffet and open-air dining allows passengers to make the most of sunny days and relaxing by the pool.

The food on offer is cooked to order, with burgers, hot dogs and steaks being the specialties. Health-conscious passengers will appreciate the selection of salads available from the buffet-style serving area.

A popular dining alternative, passengers can eat their food in a quintessential cruising atmosphere, under blue skies, whilst taking in the view of both the Lido Pool and the ocean.

THE VERANDAH

Named for the first-class Verandah Grills found aboard Cunard's original *Queen Mary* and *Queen Elizabeth*, The Verandah is an alternative dining venue aboard *Queen Elizabeth*.

Located on Deck 2, just off the Grand Lobby, the restaurant offers a distinctive French menu that will be talked about long after guests depart the ship. The ingredients used to prepare the dishes from this menu are of the highest quality and many of them are imported from France and sent to the ship, even when she is on extended cruises.

A light and airy room with artwork inspired by the murals on the first two Queens, the room aims to recreate the dining experience on board the original *Queen Elizabeth*.

Open for both lunch and dinner service, this extra tariff restaurant is a popular dining choice for both new and repeat guests and bookings are essential.

DID YOU KNOW?

The Verandah's menu was created by Cunard culinary ambassador Jean-Marie Zimmermann.

BARS AND LOUNGES

Elegant spaces to relax and discuss shipboard life with fellow guests over a drink abound on *Queen Elizabeth*. The ship offers indoor and outdoor bars, a casino, a traditional-style pub, a show lounge and a nightclub.

The bars and lounges aboard provide comfortable seating by day and night, as well as a wide selection of drinks and regular entertainment.

BAR PROFILES

BAR NAME	LOCATION
Grills Lounge	Deck 11
Commodore Club	Deck 10
The Admiral's Lounge	Deck 10
Churchill's Cigar Lounge	Deck 10
The Yacht Club	Deck 10
The Garden Lounge	Deck 9
Pavilion Bar	Deck 9
Lido Pool Bar	Deck 9
Midships Bar	Deck 3
Card Room	Deck 3
Empire Casino	Deck 2
Golden Lion	Deck 2
Queens Room	Deck 2
Café Carinthia	Deck 2
Royal Court Theatre	Deck 1, 2 & 3

GRILLS LOUNGE

DID YOU KNOW?

Queen Elizabeth's call sign was G.B.T.T., which was the same as *QE2* and RMS *Queen Mary*. It was changed to ZCEF2 when the ship was re-registered in Bermuda.

The Grills Lounge on Deck 11 is set aside for the exclusive use of Grills passengers. The lounge is located at the top of a private stairway and between the two Grill restaurants.

The focal point of the Grills Lounge is the leaded glass ceiling which is illuminated at all times from above. Comfortable couches and chairs are arranged around the room for the relaxation of guests.

COMMODORE CLUB

The Commodore Club has a strong nautical theme with images of ships from days gone by adorning the walls. The fixtures of the room are Art Deco in design and the windows which look out over the bow of the ship are arranged in a pleasing curved design.

The Commodore Club is an excellent place to relax during the day as it offers comfortable chairs in which to sit in the sun, without the risk of overheating or burning that is inherent in sitting on the deck. This lounge is also a fantastic place to enjoy the experience of entering or leaving ports, especially when the weather is unfavourable for standing outside.

The Commodore Club is located at the forward end of Deck 10.

QUEEN ELIZABETH
HAMILTON

THE ADMIRAL'S LOUNGE

The Admiral's Lounge on Deck 10 is a relaxed and elegant space. It is most often used as an organised meeting space or additional concierge area for Grills passengers.

The lounge is comfortable and quiet with spectacular ocean views over the starboard side of the ship.

The '*Queen Elizabeth* Live' daily programme is filmed here, with a special film crew. Guests range from the captain to insights lecturers. The show, hosted by the Entertainment Director, is played on the in-cabin TVs during the day and explains all the goings-on aboard the ship for the day.

CHURCHILL'S CIGAR LOUNGE

Churchill's Cigar Lounge is located on Deck 10 on the starboard side, just behind the Admiral's Lounge. The cigar lounge is one of the few public spaces aboard where pipe and cigar smoking is allowed.

Churchill's Cigar Lounge is a quiet area with an elegant atmosphere and is decorated with wood panelling and images of Sir Winston Churchill, who was a regular traveller aboard the first Cunard Queens.

THE YACHT CLUB

Situated high atop the ship on Deck 10 you'll find The Yacht Club, *Queen Elizabeth*'s nightclub bar. Named for the much-loved bar aboard predecessor *QE2*, The Yacht Club features a spectacular chandelier centred over its circular dance floor.

Former *QE2* passengers will be happy to see the famous silver *QE2* model (created by Asprey's in the early 1970s) displayed at the entrance to this room. The model, a priceless piece of Cunard memorabilia, was originally displayed in *QE2*'s Midships Lobby.

A quiet lounge by day, the room is in its element after dark, with DJ music, dancing and drinks available until the wee hours.

DID YOU KNOW?

The signal flags near the ceiling of The Yacht Club spell out '*Queen Elizabeth 2* Triumph of a great tradition 1969-2008'.

THE GARDEN LOUNGE

Amidships on Deck 9 is the Garden Lounge. As the name suggests, this room has a garden theme, with padded wicker furniture and plants arranged around the space. The glass ceiling provides a fantastic amount of light during daylight hours whilst protecting occupants from fickle weather.

In the evening the Garden Lounge offers occasional supper clubs, for those wishing to dine and dance under the stars. When not in use for this purpose it is open to all and is a great place to enjoy an evening's relaxation.

The Garden Lounge bar is located on the port side of the room and has Art Deco stools for guests to sit on whilst watching the bar staff compound their cocktail of choice. The room also contains a small stage for musical performances. The Garden Lounge is located directly between the Pavilion Pool area and the Lido restaurant.

PAVILION BAR

Asked of the barman in the Pavilion Bar:

'When you go off duty tonight, how do you get home?'

The Pavilion Bar serves drinks to thirsty sunbathers at the forward end of the Pavilion Pool. The bar is covered, as it is located under the overhanging deck above.

With lounges and tables arranged along the covered area by the windows enclosing the Pavilion Pool, this bar is a great place to sit and enjoy the day in the sun or out of it.

LIDO POOL BAR

On the aft of Deck 9 is the Lido Pool area and Lido Pool Bar. Those wishing to partake in a drink whilst sitting by the Lido Pool or enjoying the view of the ship's wake will frequent this bar.

The bar is wood panelled with wooden bar stools for those who wish to sit upright. Other passengers may prefer to lounge on one of the many deckchairs located in this area. During her five-year refit, special awnings were added to this deck to provide extra shelter and shade.

THE PINA COLADA

One part white rum
One part coconut cream
Three parts pineapple juice
Blend with ice until smooth. Pour into chilled glass, garnish and serve.

MIDSHIPS BAR

On Deck 3 running along the starboard side of the Grand Lobby is the Midships Bar. In the forward part of the bar, tables and chairs are arranged by the windows and look out over the Promenade Deck. The aft part of the bar is designated the Veuve Clicquot Champagne Bar and has a darker aspect as there are no windows in this part of the bar.

Curved railings divide the bar area from the corridor. The curved theme is repeated in the shape of the actual bar and provides a pleasing aspect to the room.

The Midships Bar contains a number of cabinets with memorabilia and other objects celebrating the heritage of the original Cunard *Queen Elizabeth*, including an impressive model of that ship.

DID YOU KNOW?

The map displayed in the Midships Bar is a replica of the one aboard RMS *Queen Mary* in the first-class dining room. The original mural had a model of the ship that was moved to indicate the progress made by the ship during her crossing.

CARD ROOM

Passengers can brush up on their card skills, learn new ones or put their skills to the test in the Card Room located on the port side of Deck 3.

This room is wood panelled and is set up specifically for the purpose of card games. At the entrance to the room is a tiled half circle depicting the four suits: clubs, diamonds, hearts and spades. There are more than twenty tables, each allowing four challengers to partake in a variety of games.

Regular bridge and whist sessions are held during cruises. These sessions arc run by the entertainment staff and are extremely popular, resulting in the room often filling to capacity!

EMPIRE CASINO

A very popular venue on board *Queen Elizabeth* is the Empire Casino, located on Deck 2. As the name indicates, this is the place to go if you wish to try your hand at blackjack, roulette or on the poker machines.

The Empire Casino is a stylish location. The backlit glass insets in the ceiling, combined with the stylised pillars, create a very distinct feel. The casino is open only when the ship is at sea, as regulations stipulate that it cannot open in port.

GOLDEN LION

If you have a hankering for traditional pub-style food then the Golden Lion on Deck 2 is the place to go. The Golden Lion provides a relaxed and welcoming environment to sample the pub lunch menu, enjoy a drink and experience live music.

The bar serves ale on tap, as well as a variety of beverages from around the world. The room hosts entertainment favourites including quizzes and karaoke, and also provides a link to the outside world with televisions showing sports and news.

QUEENS ROOM

In our busy everyday lives there is rarely the time or opportunity to indulge in some of the pleasanter customs of former years. Not so in the Queens Room on Deck 2.

High tea is served daily from 3.30 to 4.30 p.m. and the room quickly fills up as guests take advantage of the opportunity to be served dainty sandwiches and cakes by white-gloved wait staff.

In addition to the high tea ritual, the Queens Room is also the venue for classical music performances and bingo games. In the evening, music and dance hosts are provided for

those wishing to take to the dance floor. Some nights are even designated as ball nights, with the room decorated to suit the theme of the ball. Every night in the Queens Room live music is provided courtesy of one of the ship's bands.

Though the room is located on Deck 2, there are great views of the room to be had from Deck 3 as the area over the dance floor is open to the deck above. This double-height ceiling provides the perfect foil for the two chandeliers that hang over the dance floor.

CAFÉ CARINTHIA

A popular pre-dinner drinks location for Britannia and Britannia Club passengers, Café Carinthia is located just forward of the Britannia Club restaurant. Based on the room aboard *Queen Victoria*, this bar offers a relaxed and cosy atmosphere to sit at any time of day.

Café Carinthia serves tea and coffee throughout the day, with sandwiches, rolls and quiches available over the lunch hours. True to Cunard tradition, cakes and tarts are supplied for afternoon tea.

In the evening canapés and bar snacks are offered, as passengers enjoy the elegant evening atmosphere and take in the interior view towards the Grand Lobby.

ROYAL COURT THEATRE

Located over three decks at the forward end of the ship is the Royal Court Theatre. Those on stage are able to see their audience of nearly 800 passengers seated on two levels and in the ship's sixteen theatre boxes. The first theatre boxes at sea were introduced in 2007 aboard *Queen Victoria* and their success has resulted in them being included on *Queen Elizabeth*. The theatre boxes are available to anyone on a

DID YOU KNOW?

Queen Elizabeth has its own theatre company who stage a number of production shows on every voyage.

first-come, first-served basis for most shows, lectures and other presentations. On production show nights, the boxes come into their own, featuring bell boy escorts, sparkling wine and chocolates for those passengers who have opted to pre-book for this royal treatment.

In addition to hosting presentations, lectures, musical performances and after-dinner entertainment, the Royal Court Theatre is also the location where classic and new-release films are shown. A large screen is dropped down behind the stage when required.

ENTERTAINMENT ON BOARD

Life aboard the early Cunard ships was fairly basic, with limited amenities and facilities. Passengers were left to entertain themselves during the long voyage across the Atlantic. However, as ships grew in size, amenities improved and Cunard pioneered such facilities as music rooms, writing rooms and gentlemen's smoking rooms.

By the 1940s the original Queens, *Mary* and *Elizabeth*, boasted their own first-class cinema, swimming pools and Turkish baths. However, the majority of passengers still entertained themselves after dinner with conversation, drinks and strolls around the deck.

Though these activities are still available, Cunard's current *Queen Elizabeth* offers many other entertainment options.

Throughout the ship the entertainment staff can be found hosting bingo in the Queens Room, karaoke in the Golden Lion pub, deck sports, art and craft activities – the list goes on! Guests are kept informed of what activities are available by a daily programme, printed aboard and delivered each evening to all staterooms. The daily programme details times and locations of organised activities, as well as providing suggestions to fill all other waking moments.

ALASTAIR GREENER WAS QUEEN ELIZABETH'S FIRST ENTERTAINMENT DIRECTOR:

Cunard is very proud of being a company with over 170 years of experience; enjoying innovation and setting new industry standards. With a department of nearly a hundred, the *Queen Elizabeth* entertainment team has introduced contemporary and exciting new developments to the on-board entertainment programme with the latest addition to the Cunard fleet.

During the day *Queen Elizabeth* offers Cunard's award-winning Insights enrichment programme which introduces guests to stimulating experts and accomplished academics, through a series of lectures.

The latest Cunarder also boasts a brand new Games Deck, which was inspired by an area on the first *Queen Elizabeth*. The ship is now able to offer our guests short mat bowls and croquet in addition to fencing and the traditional games such as shuffleboard, quoits and paddle tennis.

The Queens Room is an iconic space for Cunard and brings a wonderful sense of grandeur to the ship and it's where guests enjoy white-gloved afternoon tea service, dance classes, lectures and even classical concerts. In the evening the venue really shines as one of only three ballrooms at sea. It plays host to Cunard's famous Royal Nights, with a resident orchestra, vocalist and gentlemen dance hosts. *Queen Elizabeth* has maintained the traditions set by her sisters, but has added new themes such as the Elizabethan Ball, the Starlight Ball and the London Ball.

In the stunning three-deck Royal Court Theatre, featuring sixteen private boxes, another new concept has been introduced. With the newly formed *Queen Elizabeth* Theatre Company, guests enjoy a brand new repertoire of shows premiered by the Company's twenty-one singers, dancers and actors.

As *Queen Elizabeth*'s first Entertainment Director, I am very proud to present this new concept of entertainment at sea, where yet again Cunard introduces innovative ideas, which sets a new standard of on-board entertainment.

Alastair Greener

March 2011

PUBLIC ROOMS

Leisure activities aboard *Queen Elizabeth* are not limited to what is found in the bars and lounges. There are a number of locations around the ship that have been designed to allow passengers to enjoy a varied entertainment schedule.

The ship offers gym and spa facilities that are world class, high-end shopping, a library, historical images and artefacts and internet access, as well as entertainment that caters specifically to under-eighteens.

Passengers should have no trouble finding something to do. The only difficulty will be deciding what should be done first!

PLAY ZONE

Kids will love the cruising experience aboard *Queen Elizabeth*, with a dedicated Play Zone located on Deck 10.

While parents will rejoice in the opportunity for some time alone, their children will be enjoying fun-filled activities including outdoor games, puzzles and mazes.

With both an indoor and outdoor play area, the Play Zone is available for passengers aged 1-12, and parents will be able to relax with the knowledge that their children are being cared for by qualified nannies.

THE ZONE

Strictly for those guests aged between 12 and 18, The Zone on Deck 10 offers entertainments and activities that will leave older guests wishing they could wind back the sands of time!

With space to meet and socialise with others of a similar age, The Zone is fitted out with multiple gaming devices, including Nintendo Wiis and Sony Playstations, as well as an air hockey table, home theatre and foosball.

Teens can participate in planned group events, watch movies or just chill out on the comfortable couches in The Zone.

CUNARD HEALTH CLUB & SPA

Keeping on top of your fitness and beauty regimens whilst at sea is no hardship aboard *Queen Elizabeth*. The Cunard Health Club & Spa, located at the forward end of Decks 9 and 10, offers excellent facilities with unbeatable views.

The fitness area with cardio and weight equipment is located on the forward end of Deck 9, with windows overlooking the bow of the ship. Treatment rooms for various relaxation therapies are situated aft and above the gym, with the hydrotherapy pool located just forward of the Pavilion Pool in an enclosed area.

In addition to offering a number of different massage techniques and sauna facilities, the spa also offers beauty treatments including manicures, hair treatments and teeth whitening.

ROYAL ARCADE

They say that diamonds are a girl's best friend, but they are not the only thing for sale in the Royal Arcade. Located on Deck 3, the Royal Arcade is an attractive shopping area, with stores located around a central void and a great view of the grand staircase rising from the Deck 2 lobby below.

The shops aboard *Queen Elizabeth* sell designer perfumes, jewellery and accessories. In addition there is a shop specialising in Cunard merchandise, including clothing, bags and hats. Glass frontage and period design make the Royal Arcade worth a visit if only for the pleasure of the scenery.

CUNARD

FORTNUM & MASON

Located on Deck 3 just forward of the Midships Bar is Fortnum & Mason. Offering all of the conveniences of home, items for sale vary from basics, such as toiletries, to branded items perfect for gifts.

For those on longer voyages, one of the delights of Fortnum & Mason is the varied supply of well-known chocolate bars, including Mars, Cadbury's and Galaxy.

CLARENDON'S ART GALLERY & CUNARDER'S GALLERY

Adjacent to the Queens Room balcony is Clarendon's Art Gallery. This gallery shows art works which are available to buy throughout the voyage. Art works purchased aboard the ship can be delivered to the purchaser's home, eliminating the difficulty of transporting extra luggage home at the end of the journey.

Also on Deck 3, located slightly aft of the main art gallery, is Clarendon's Cunarder's Gallery. The Cunarder's Gallery displays framed Cunard prints including marketing posters and photographs of famous travellers of days gone by.

The prints on display in the Cunarder's Gallery are also for sale aboard the ship and are an ideal souvenir of your voyage on the historic line.

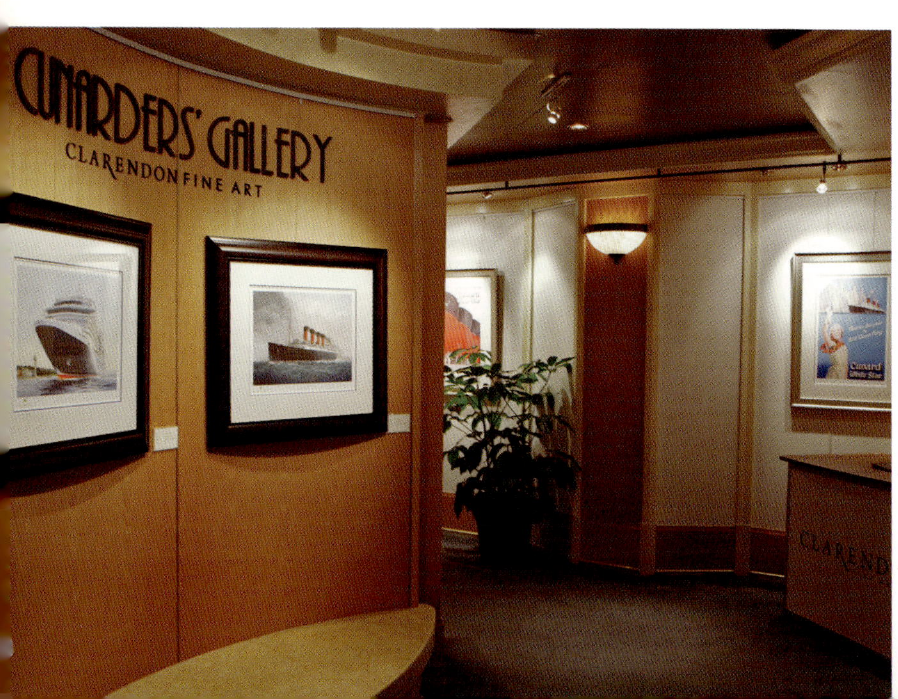

IMAGES PHOTO GALLERY

It is said that a picture is worth a thousand words and Images on *Queen Elizabeth* is the place to buy photographic memories of your trip.

The ship sails with a team of professional photographers aboard who are on hand to capture special moments. Occasions captured in photographic form, including boarding, your arrival in new ports and formal nights, are popular mementos and can be viewed and purchased from Images on Deck 3.

In addition to the personalised photos on sale, there is also a collection of stock photos of the ship in various ports available for purchase, as well as historic images from the Cunard archives.

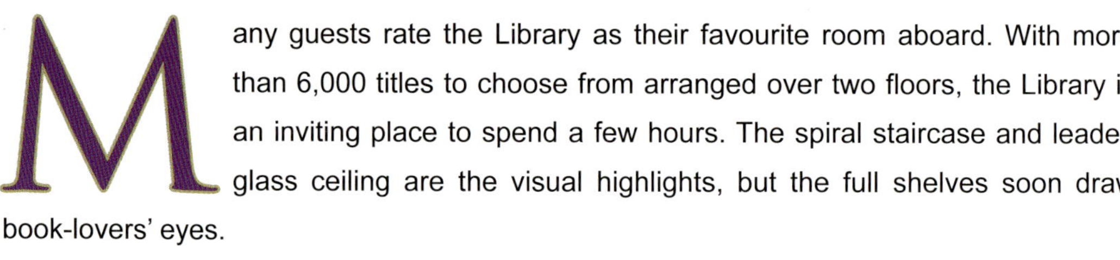

LIBRARY

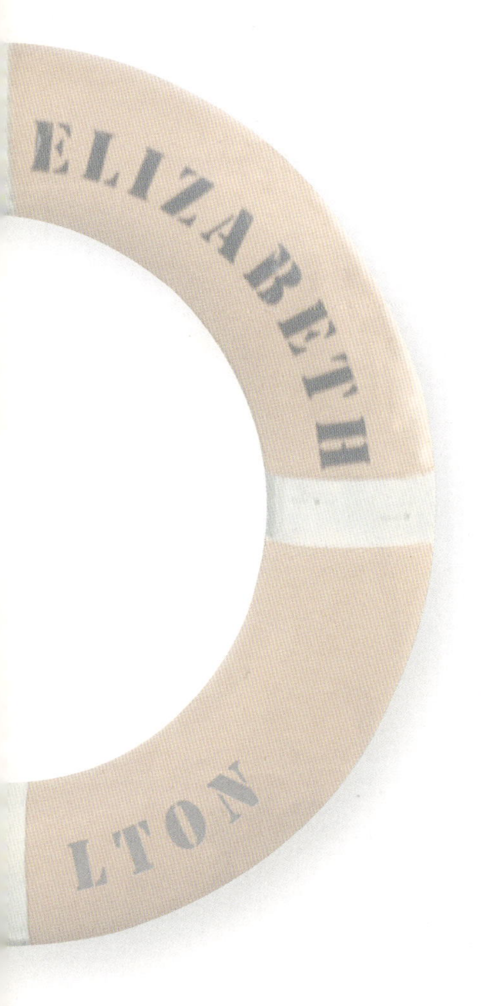

Many guests rate the Library as their favourite room aboard. With more than 6,000 titles to choose from arranged over two floors, the Library is an inviting place to spend a few hours. The spiral staircase and leaded glass ceiling are the visual highlights, but the full shelves soon draw book-lovers' eyes.

Most books can be checked out and read at leisure around the ship. Some titles, in particular those relating to the next port to be visited, are restricted to the Library, and passengers can relax on the leather chairs within the confines of this multi-levelled room to brush up on local knowledge before arriving at their next port of call.

QUEEN
ELIZABETH
HAMI
LTON

EXIT

BOOK SHOP

Books abound in *Queen Elizabeth*'s Book Shop, located on Deck 2, starboard. An impressive selection of maritime books is the main feature here; however, if you are looking for fiction, travel guides or other general interest books the Book Shop is sure to be satisfying.

If it is memorabilia, mementos or gifts that you're looking for, the Book Shop has an extensive selection of items to choose from. Popular gifts include *Queen Elizabeth* bookmarks, pens, posters and postcards for you to share with friends and family at home.

With its quiet atmosphere and friendly staff, the Book Shop is bound to be a popular destination aboard during your cruise.

INTERNET CENTRE

The Internet Centre on Deck 1 offers passengers an easy way to stay in touch with family and friends at home.

Internet access is provided for a fee and passengers can use the computers located in the Internet Centre and ConneXions 1.

Guests with their own laptop or tablet computers will enjoy the WiFi service found throughout *Queen Elizabeth*. Setting this up is simple and affords passengers the ability to stay in touch with the outside world without having to leave their favourite chair.

CONNEXIONS

While most people travel purely for pleasure, there are those who travel for business reasons, and others who like to seek out new skills while on holiday.

For this purpose *Queen Elizabeth* has three rooms named ConneXions. ConneXions 1 is located on Deck 1 off the Grand Lobby. This room serves as a secondary Internet Centre and is equipped with iMac computers. Specialist assistants are on hand to teach guests how to use the latest Apple products.

On Deck 3, just aft of the Queens Room promenade, you will find ConneXions 2 and 3. These rooms can be set up to accommodate meetings and conferences as required, offering excellent flexibility for those who are working while at sea.

TOUR OFFICE

If you didn't book your shore excursions before you left home, don't despair! The Tour Office is here to help.

Situated on Deck 1 on the lower level of the Grand Lobby, a team of travel and tour experts are on hand to assist you in organising tours at all of your ports of call.

Once tours are booked, tickets are delivered direct to your cabin. Tickets must be taken to the pre-assigned meeting place on the day of your tour, details of which are published in the daily programme.

PURSER'S DESK

The shipboard reception and concierge service can be found at the Purser's Desk, situated on Deck 1 near the Grand Lobby.

The Purser's Desk staff are often the first members of *Queen Elizabeth*'s crew that passengers see, as they oversee the embarkation process.

From directions to help you find your way around the ship to foreign exchange, the team at the Purser's Desk are available to help you with every question you might have. Manned 24 hours a day, you can access information here any time of day or night either by visiting the desk or calling them direct from your cabin.

DID YOU KNOW?

The Purser's Desk handles all mail aboard the ship and even stamps postcards and letters with special 'Posted aboard *Queen Elizabeth*' stamps!

GETTING THERE

Thanks to a logical interior design that is based upon three major stairways, it is easy to find your way around *Queen Elizabeth*. The three passenger stairways are labelled A to C from forward to aft and link all decks aboard the ship.

Despite the simplicity of her design, there are a myriad of corridors to explore aboard linking all passenger staterooms with the major public rooms. Many of the stairways and corridors are decorated with paintings of historic Cunarders.

MEMORABILIA DÉJÀ VU

When *QE2* was retired in 2008 most of the memorabilia aboard the ship went with her to her new home of Dubai. A number of pieces have since been returned to Cunard on loan and are on display in various locations around *Queen Elizabeth*.

Pieces from *QE2* include the gold bust of HM Queen Elizabeth II, the Royal Standards found in the Queens Room, as well as *QE2*'s Bell and Builders Plaque located outside the Commodore Club. A silver model of *QE2* is also on loan, displayed in The Yacht Club.

ART ABOARD

The on-board art collection pays homage to the classic Cunarders of yesteryear. There is an extensive collection of maritime art, including paintings of legendary Cunard liners such as *Mauretania*, *Aquitania*, *Berengaria* and the original Queens.

QE2 features heavily aboard the latest Elizabeth, with many paintings, photographs and artefacts of the famed Cunarder scattered about the corridors and stairways.

In addition there are a number of art works that have been commissioned for the latest *Queen Elizabeth*, including the ship's portrait on Deck 1 of the Grand Lobby and a portrait of HM Queen Elizabeth II on Deck 3 of the Grand Lobby, painted by Isobel Peachey.

DID YOU KNOW?

The portrait of HM Queen Elizabeth II was unveiled at a private event at the National Portrait Gallery in London.

ON DECK

One of the great benefits of travelling by ship is the luxury of time to do nothing. *Queen Elizabeth*'s open deck areas are the perfect place to enjoy some time to yourself. Deckchairs are located around the ship and many passengers take advantage of them, whether to soak up some sun, read a book, watch the ocean or even take a nap.

If you are feeling in need of a more energetic pastime you may find what you're looking for on the Games Deck or at the Pavilion or Lido Pools. Joining the deck parties which are held to celebrate sailaways and sometimes just the warm weather are another great way to enjoy the deck space.

COPY THAT!

The *Queen Elizabeth* is a large ship spanning nearly 294m long and has twelve decks to explore. To overcome the possibility of getting lost, some passengers have been known to walk around the vessel with walkie-talkies to keep in contact with their friends and families elsewhere on the ship.

TERRACE & COURTYARD

DID YOU KNOW?

While the plants and flowers inside the ship are all real, those located on deck are plastic. This is because customs regulations at many ports prohibit any material that may carry bugs or diseases from making contact with the local environment.

The Terrace and Courtyard are open deck areas for the exclusive use of those travelling Queens or Princess Grill.

The Courtyard is located on Deck 11 directly between the Queens Grill and Princess Grill restaurants. Passengers can choose to dine here, in more casual and airy surroundings. Though open to the sky, the Courtyard is sheltered from wind by the walls of the restaurants and the funnel casing.

The Terrace and Upper Terrace are used mainly for sunbathing. The Terrace is accessible both from the Grills Lounge and also from the open deck below. The Upper Terrace can be reached from the Courtyard or from the private Grills staircase and lifts.

The Upper Terrace is the closest passengers can get to the funnel and the highest passenger area aboard the ship.

GAMES DECK

On the forward end of Deck 11 you will find the Games Deck. This area can be accessed by the twin staircases which lead up from outside The Yacht Club or by the A staircase and lift.

The Games Deck offers a covered area with designated courts in which to play paddle tennis, croquet and bowls. Directly above The Yacht Club is a giant chess board for those who prefer a mental workout to a physical one.

Traditional shipboard games, such as deck quoits and shuffleboard, can be played on the areas of Deck 10 immediately next to the stairs leading up to the Games Deck.

DID YOU KNOW?

The three coins displayed on the Games Deck wall commemorate the launch of the three *Queen Elizabeth*s. One is dated 1938, one 1967 and the third 2010.

PAVILION POOL

Swimmers will love the Pavilion Pool situated atop *Queen Elizabeth* on Deck 9.

Those wishing to keep fit during their voyage are often seen swimming here in the early morning while most passengers are still sleeping.

Sheltered on both sides by large glass windows and long enough to swim laps, the pool area is open to the sky allowing for an indoor/outdoor atmosphere.

Nearby the Pavilion Bar, the pool area is sometimes used for evening parties, including dancing to the music of the ship's band.

LIDO POOL

Located at the very aft of Deck 9, the Lido Pool is accessible via the Lido Restaurant and offers bathers supreme views over the stern of the ship.

The surrounding deck area holds a vast number of deckchairs and sun beds, affording those on vacation a chance to soak up a bit of sun as the ship makes her way from port to port.

Here passengers can marvel at the endless blue of the ocean, interrupted only by *Queen Elizabeth*'s wake – one of the many joys of cruising.

Catered by its own eatery, the Lido Pool area is popular on Mediterranean and Caribbean cruises.

DID YOU KNOW?

Since 2011, Queen Elizabeth has been registered in Hamilton, Bermuda (previously it was Southampton).

PROMENADE DECK

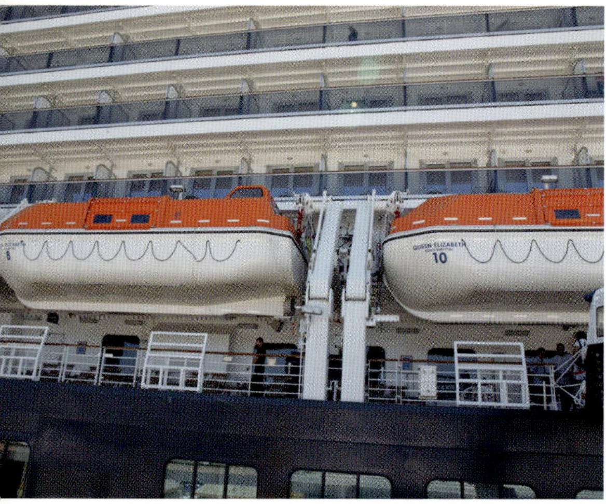

Whether you prefer to run, jog, walk or simply to sit and watch the world go by, the Promenade Deck is the place for you.

Situated on Deck 3, the Promenade Deck runs around the ship with fantastic views from both the port and starboard sides, whilst the stern offers unrivalled views of *Queen Elizabeth*'s wake.

Here you'll find traditional wooden steamer chairs which offer the illusion that you've stepped back in time, perhaps to the 1920s aboard such iconic liners as *Mauretania* or *Aquitania*.

The Promenade Deck offers passengers shelter from the elements thanks to the lifeboats which are suspended above the deck.

EXTERIOR

There is no more recognisable fleet than the ships of the Cunard Line. Dressed in a livery that dates back to the first Cunard ship (*Britannia* of 1840), *Queen Elizabeth* sports a black hull with white superstructure, making her stand out among other cruise ships which are usually painted completely white.

The elegance of Cunard's livery is supported by the stylised white mast and *QE2*-inspired funnel painted in the traditional black and red. This gives the ship an elegant appearance while still allowing her to appear modern.

DID YOU KNOW?

The colour 'Cunard Red' was created by Robert Napier in 1840. He was searching for a paint that could withstand the intense heat produced by the smokestacks of Cunard's first ship, RMS *Britannia*. A mixture of bright ochre and buttermilk was applied. With the heat of the smokestacks, the paint mixture literally 'cooked' on to the stacks and stayed put.

Bottom Right: **(Courtesy of John Frame)**

THE ELIZABETHS

Travelling aboard *Queen Elizabeth*, you'll find yourself part of a grand tradition that started with the first Cunard *Queen Elizabeth* of 1940. When built she was, at over 85,000 gross tons, the largest passenger ship ever – a title she held until 1996 when finally eclipsed by the 100,000-gross-ton *Carnival Destiny*.

Her successor, *QE2*, was purposely built smaller than the previous Queens. This allowed her to transit the Panama Canal. To reduce her draft, she was lightened by using aluminium on her superstructure and this also allowed for her to be one deck taller than her predecessor.

Today's *Queen Elizabeth* is the second largest Cunarder ever built (after *QM2*). While her length is similar to *QE2*'s (allowing her to transit the Panama Canal), she is far larger in terms of gross tonnage.

Above: The ship's builders' plate showing yard number 6178.
Right: *QE2* of 1969.
Opposite, left: *Queen Elizabeth* of 1940. (Simplon Post Cards)
Opposite, right: Bust of HM The Queen.

QUEEN ELIZABETH COMPARISON CHART

	Queen Elizabeth (1940)	*Queen Elizabeth 2* (1969)	*Queen Elizabeth* (2010)
Tonnage	83,673 GRT	70,327 GRT (1994-)	90,400 GRT
Length	314m (1,031ft)	293.5m (963ft)	294m (964ft)
Width	36m (118ft)	32m (105ft)	32.3m (106ft)
Draft	12m (38ft)	9.7m (32ft)	8m (26ft)
Speed	28 knots	32.5 knots	23.7 knots
Passengers	2,283 people	1,777 people	2,092 people
Crew	1,000 people	1,040 people	996 people

THE FUNNEL

High atop the ship, located just aft of the Courtyard you'll find *Queen Elizabeth*'s funnel. The most noticeable feature of the ship, the funnel is based on a design first modelled aboard *QE2* and is dressed in the traditional Cunard colours of black and red.

The funnel consists of the smokestack, cowling and a large scoop at the base which assists in directing air upwards, disbursing smoke and soot and ensuring the aft decks remain dirt-free.

Identical to the funnel aboard *Queen Victoria*, this structure houses two of the ship's whistles as well as some of the ship's navigational lights.

THE MAST

Just atop the Bridge at the forward end of the ship is one of *Queen Elizabeth*'s signature design traits, the mast.

Like all current Cunarders, the mast aboard *Queen Elizabeth* is based on the design first introduced by *QE2* in the late 1960s.

The mast is highly stylised when compared to other modern cruise ships. It does, however, provide a functional use and houses various pieces of navigation equipment, as well as the signal flags, Cunard house flag, red ensign and courtesy flag for the port being visited.

BEHIND THE SCENES

Stepping behind the scenes aboard *Queen Elizabeth* is like stepping into another world. Stark in comparison to the Art Deco luxury of the passenger spaces, the behind-the-scenes areas are extremely functional.

Machinery, engine rooms, storerooms, galleys and crew accommodation fill the spaces not dedicated to passenger use. There are eight service elevators for crew to use, which access all areas of the ship. While there are twelve decks for passenger use, the crew have access to all sixteen decks, some of which are below the water line.

Whilst the ship sleeps at night, the behind the scenes areas are never quiet. During port days passengers can catch a glimpse of the hive of activity that usually goes unnoticed. Provisioning the ship is a busy task which involves co-ordination between the crew and the port staff.

THE BRIDGE

Situated at the forward end of Deck 8, the Bridge is the central hub of operations for *Queen Elizabeth*.

Elevated 26m above sea level with unobstructed forward-facing views, the Bridge is fully enclosed. Two Bridge Wings overhang the sides of the ship and provide those on duty with an aft view which is essential when docking or sailing in confined areas, such as the Panama Canal.

In addition to housing state-of-the-art communication equipment, the Bridge is also home to navigational aids such as radar, sonar, speed indicators and manoeuvring information.

Manned 24 hours, with two officers on watch at all times, the Bridge is a constant hive of activity as *Queen Elizabeth* sails around the globe.

COMMODORE RYND REFLECTS ON QUEEN ELIZABETH'S FIFTH ANNIVERSARY REFIT

Even though she is just coming up to her fifth birthday, *Queen Elizabeth* underwent a substantial refit in June 2014 for both routine work and enhancements. Single-berth cabins were fitted on Deck 2 using space gained from the reduction in the size of the Casino.

Her alternators were upgraded and a new one installed. New high-tech coatings were applied on the underwater hull to enable her to slip through the water with less friction and more efficiency.

Shade canopies were fitted on Deck 12, for the Grills sunbathing area, and on Deck 9, Lido Deck, to provide some shade for guests on hot days. New mattresses were fitted to every bed and new LED flat-screen televisions were installed in every stateroom and suite. Substantial areas of carpet were renewed.

So at the time of her fifth birthday *Queen Elizabeth* is better than ever, having retained all that our guests liked, as well as having added, improved or renewed much else, giving her a fresh look and feel.

Commodore Rynd, 2015

DID YOU KNOW?

Commodore Rynd has commanded all four modern Queens, including *QE2*, *QM2*, *Queen Victoria* and *Queen Elizabeth*.

Queen Elizabeth in the Bay of Biscay. (Courtesy of Commodore Rynd)
Left: Commodore Rynd. (Cunard / Commodore Rynd)

THE ENGINE ROOM

The power required to keep *Queen Elizabeth* operating is substantial and behind the scenes a dedicated team of engineers and technicians are working hard to ensure that the ship's power plant operates smoothly.

Queen Elizabeth is powered by six Caterpillar MaK M43C diesel engines which allow the ship to achieve a maximum speed of 23.7 knots. The ship is propelled by two ABB podded propellers. These pods hang under the ship like giant outboard motors and pull the ship through the water (the propeller is at the front). As they can rotate a full 360° they negate the need for a rudder, making *Queen Elizabeth* more manoeuvrable than older cruise ships.

To assist with docking procedures the ship has three Fincantieri Riva Trigoso bow thrusters. These thrusters are large shafts that run through the bow of the ship (from port to starboard) with a propeller located within the shaft. Combining these thrusters with the flexibility of the pods allows *Queen Elizabeth* to dock herself at most ports, without any assistance from tugs.

Stability at sea is an important part of the modern cruise experience. To ensure a smooth ride, the ship has two stabilisers which assist to reduce movement and thus reduce the likelihood of seasickness.

DID YOU KNOW?

Queen Elizabeth is the first Cunarder to be powered by Caterpillar engines.

ESCAPE

THE STORES

The dining experience aboard *Queen Elizabeth* is run so efficiently that passengers often forget they are aboard a ship.

The logistics required to ensure that food is available 24/7 is remarkable. Planning and food orders are completed months in advance of each voyage. Computer systems aid in ensuring the correct amount of food is ordered for each cruise. This is particularly important on longer voyages (such as the transatlantic) when the ship is at sea for seven days without ports of call.

The Stores are located below the water line, far away from passenger areas. The various storerooms and fridges include specific meat, fish, fruit and vegetable, dairy goods, dry goods and drinks rooms.

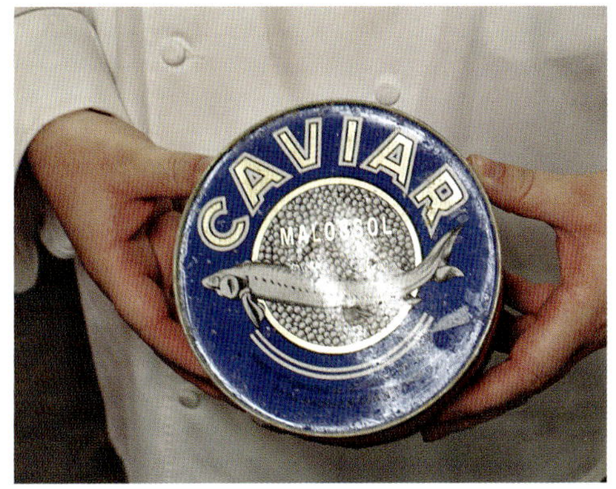

Chocolate Stores.

Champagne Stores.

Ice Cream Stores.

FOOD FACTS

Potato Stores.

Annually, *Queen Elizabeth* will use:

Tea Bags	954,681 bags
Coffee	26,789kg (59,060lb)
Eggs	1,528,707 fresh eggs
Breakfast Cereal	371,955 packs
Smoked Salmon	5,869kg (12,940lb)
Fruit Juice	109,156 litres (3,691,009oz)
Potatoes	199,721.2kg (440,310lb)
Tooth Picks	141,600
Champagne/ Sparkling	119,400 bottles
Red Wine	109,000 bottles
White Wine	119,600 bottles
Dessert Wine	3,900 bottles

Champagne Stores.

THE GALLEY

Stainless-steel benches, rows of ovens and giant hotplates are the centre of a hive of activity as over 100 chefs work in unison to ensure that every meal is an occasion to remember.

There are several galleys aboard the ship, serving the various restaurants. The largest is the Britannia Galley which produces meals for diners at the Britannia Restaurant and Britannia Club as well as *Queen Elizabeth*'s extra-tariff restaurant, The Verandah.

In addition to the Britannia Galley, there are separate galleys for the Grills and the Lido.

DID YOU KNOW?

The bakery is responsible for cooking all of the baked goods served aboard *Queen Elizabeth*. No pre-baked items are brought aboard.

The Bakery.

Bread Mixer.

Soup Cooker.

Meal-tray covers stacked up ready for dinner.

CREW ONLY

Modern cruise ships are like cities at sea, and like all cities there are many different districts. Crew areas are vast and include all the facilities and services required to keep nearly 1,000 people fed, rested and entertained while off duty.

Facilities are extensive and include a crew mess, crew bars and hundreds of cabins for accommodation. The crew aboard *Queen Elizabeth* even has exclusive use of a private sunbathing deck, found at the forward end of Deck 5.

For the officers, there is a dedicated Officers' Mess and the Officers' Wardroom, an exclusive bar for the use of the more senior members of the ship's company.

While the crew on passenger ships of days gone by had to handle months away from home with little or no communication with loved ones, the crew aboard *Queen Elizabeth* have the use of their own WiFi service, as well as an internet café.

DID YOU KNOW?

It's a tradition for the Crew Bar aboard Cunard Queens to be called 'The Pig & Whistle'.

CRUISING QUEEN

In the past twenty years the cruise industry has boomed, with more ships sailing to more destinations than ever before.

With its long heritage, it's no surprise that Cunard was one of the pioneers of the cruising vacation. In fact, it was the Cunard *Laconia* which undertook the first world cruise in history in the early 1920s.

In the late 1940s, *Caronia* became the first purpose-built Cunard cruise ship and operated an extensive cruise itinerary, carrying countless passengers around the world in unparalleled luxury.

Today, *Queen Elizabeth* continues this tradition, having undertaken her maiden world cruise during her first year of service. Throughout the year she meanders from port to port, allowing her guests the opportunity to explore destinations as historic as Venice to cities as modern as Valencia.

DID YOU KNOW?

Queen Elizabeth undertook her maiden transatlantic voyage in tandem with *Queen Victoria* in January 2011.

Right: (Courtesy of John Frame)
Opposite, lower: (Courtesy Michael Gallagher/Cunard)

QUEEN ELIZABETH
HAMI LTON

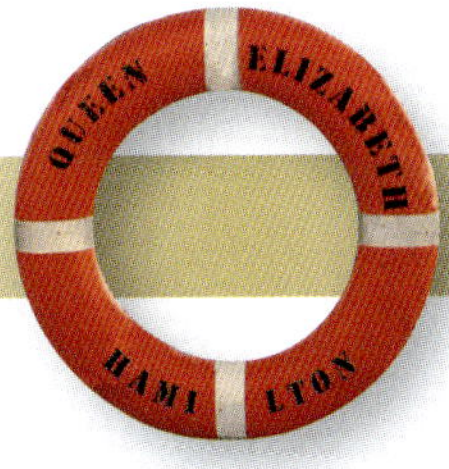

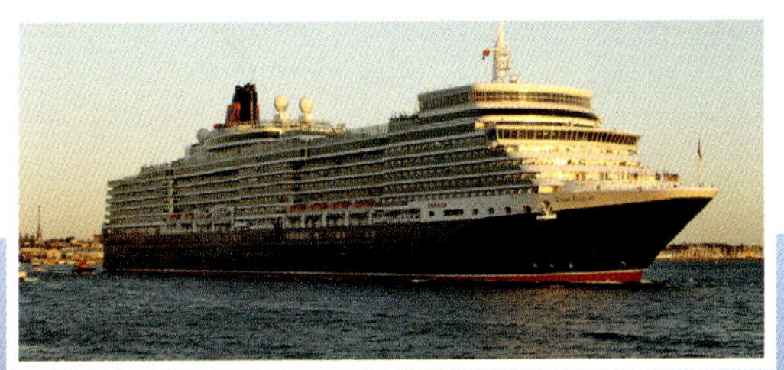

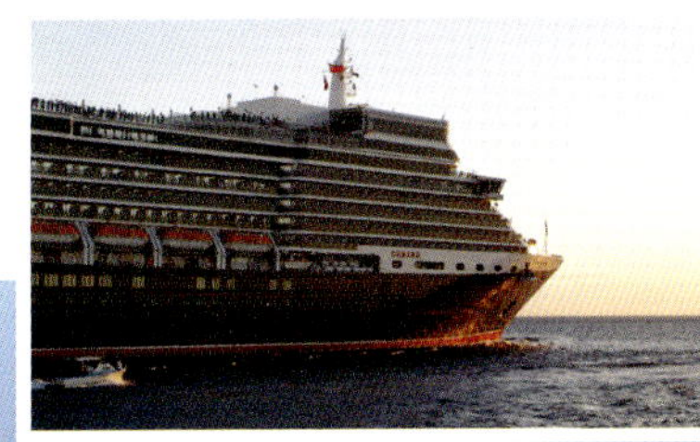

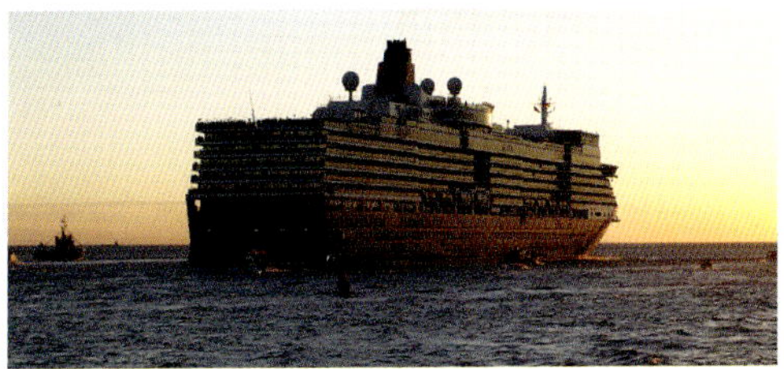

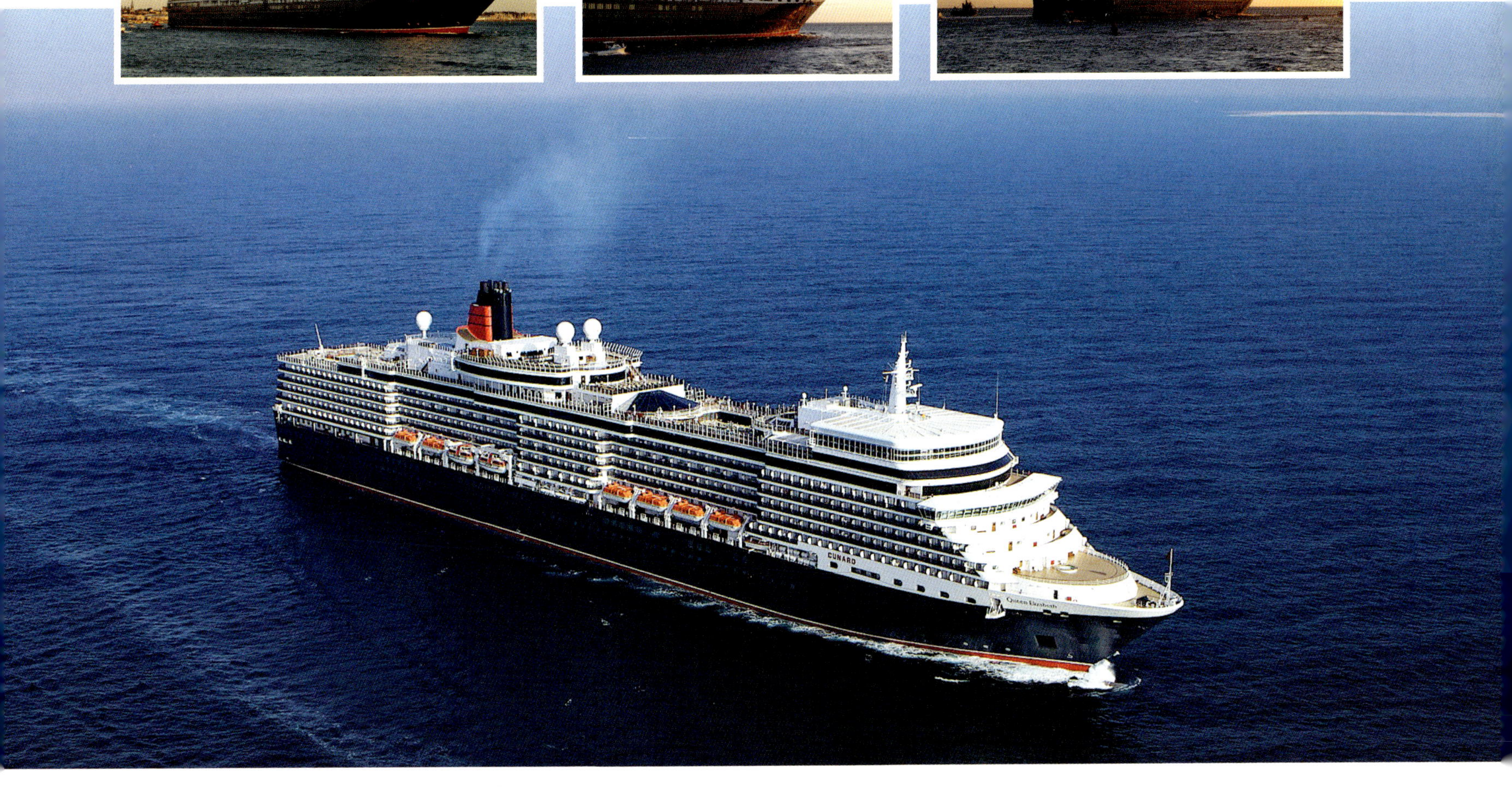
CUNARD

CAPTAIN'S PERSPECTIVE

WITH CAPTAIN CHRIS WELLS
QUEEN ELIZABETH'S FIRST MASTER

HM Queen Elizabeth II with Captain Wells. (Courtesy Michael Gallagher/Cunard)

As a twin sister to *Queen Victoria*, many will already be familiar with the silhouette and interior layout of the new *Queen Elizabeth*. However, it is the décor of the *Queen Elizabeth*, as demonstrated in this book, which makes the new ship unique, and a worthy successor to the two previous proud holders of this majestic name.

This is a modern ship, technologically advanced, with a contemporary hull, fitted with an Azipod propulsion system and powerful thrusters which permit her to be manoeuvred in ports usually without the assistance of tugs.

The passenger public spaces are spacious and light, with the double-height areas in the Britannia dining room, Grand Lobby, Queens Room and the casino adding to the ambience. Differences to her sister include a magnificent Grand Staircase between the two levels of the Britannia dining room, the elegant Garden Lounge and the additional Deck Games area on the top deck forward.

The dining areas include the superb Grills restaurants high up in the centre of the ship, with great views, incomparable food and exemplary service; the main Britannia dining room; and a new Britannia Club dining room offering single-seating dining for certain Britannia-grade staterooms.

However, it is the legacy of the 170 years of Cunard history, and particularly the heritage of the two previous bearers of the name *Queen Elizabeth*, that makes this ship really special. The original *Queen Elizabeth* was an icon of Art Deco design, and the interiors of the new ship repeat this theme in tribute to her forbear. There is a consistency of design, artwork and colour schemes through the ship which ties all the public areas together seamlessly. The new Verandah restaurant is named after the famous Verandah Grill on the original *Queen Elizabeth*.

The *Queen Elizabeth 2* is remembered on board the new ship in artwork and memorabilia, from the golden bust of Her Majesty in the Queens Room, to the glorious silver model by Asprey's of London, which is displayed centre stage in The Yacht Club.

What differentiates the Cunard liners, though, is the famous White Star Service provided by the ship's company. *Queen Elizabeth* was fortunate at delivery to be provided with experienced officers and crew taken from both *Queen Mary 2* and *Queen Victoria*, who were able to deliver this legendary service from day one.

To be given command of *Queen Elizabeth* is, of course, an honour. To lead such a ship's company is a privilege, and to stand beside the reigning monarch as she named the latest ship to bear her name was a moment of great pride.

I congratulate Chris and Rachelle on this book and hope that it inspires readers to take a voyage with us. To those reading it as they cross the oceans, I wish Bon Voyage.

Captain Chris Wells
Master, *Queen Elizabeth*

Queen Elizabeth in Southampton. (Courtesy John Hargreaves)

QUEEN ELIZABETH FACTS

Gross Registered Tonnage:	90,401 gross tons
Length:	294m/964.5ft
Beam:	32.3m/106ft
Draft:	7.9m/25.9ft
Height:	54.5m/ 179ft
Passengers:	2,092
Crew:	996
Number of Decks:	12 (Including Deck 'A')
Staterooms:	1,007

GLOSSARY OF NAUTICAL (AND QUEEN ELIZABETH) TERMS

Abeam	Off the side of the ship, at a 90° angle to its length.
Aft	Near or towards the back of the ship.
Amidships	Towards the middle of the ship.
Azimuth Pod	A propeller pod that can be rotated in any horizontal direction.
Blue Riband	Award presented for the fastest North Atlantic crossing.
Bow	The forward-most part of a ship.
Bow Thrusters	Propeller tubes that run through the width of the ship (at the bow) to help manoeuvrability.
Bridge	Navigational command centre of the ship.
Colours	The national flag or emblem flown by the ship.
Draft	Depth of water measured from the surface of the water to the ship's keel.
Forward	Near or towards the front of the ship.
Hove to	When the ship is at open sea and not moving.
Hull	The body of the vessel that stretches from the keel to the superstructure (*Queen Elizabeth*'s is painted black).
Keel	The lowest point of a vessel.
Knot	One nautical mile per hour (1 nautical mile = 1,852m or 1.15 statute miles).
Leeward	The direction away from the wind.

Ocean Liner A ship that undertakes a scheduled ocean service from point A to point B.

Pitch The alternate rise and fall of the ship which may be evident when at sea.

Pods Like giant outboard motors – the pods hang under the ship and provide propulsion, replacing the traditional propeller shafts.

Port The left side of the ship when facing forward.

Quartermaster The helmsman.

Starboard The right side of the ship when facing forward.

Stern The rearmost part of a vessel.

Superstructure The body of the ship above the main deck or hull (*Queen Elizabeth*'s is painted white).

Tender A small vessel (sometimes a lifeboat) used to transport passengers from ship to shore.

Wake The trail of disturbed water left behind the ship when it is moving.

Windward Direction the wind is blowing.

(Courtesy of Jan Frame)

BIBLIOGRAPHY

BOOKS

Braynard, F.O. and Miller, W.H. (1991), *Picture History of the Cunard Line*, Dover, United Kingdom.

Grant, R.G.. (2007), *Flight: The Complete History*, Dorling Kindersley Limited, United Kingdom.

Miller, W.H. (2001), *Picture History of British Ocean Liners: 1900 to the Present*, Dover, United Kingdom.

Miller, W.H. (1995), *Pictorial Encyclopaedia of Ocean Liners 1860-1994*, Dover, United Kingdom.

Cunard Line (2011), *Queen Elizabeth* On-board Promotional Material (Various Versions).

Cunard Line (2011), *Queen Elizabeth*: Technical and Bridge Facts (Various Versions).

PERSONAL CONVERSATIONS

Captain Chris Wells

Captain Julian Burgess

Commodore Christopher Rynd

First Engineer Petar Nikolov

Entertainment Director Alistair Greener

Executive Chef Nicholas Oldroyd

Social Hostess Freda Singleton

Cunard Historian Michael Gallagher

WEBSITES

Chris' Cunard Page: http://www.chriscunard.com/

Cunard's Official UK Homepage: http://www.cunard.co.uk/

Cunard's Official US Homepage: http://www.cunard.com/

***Queen Elizabeth* sails into the sunset from Fremantle port.**